A Symphony Of Moments

Life's Notes

Shardul Narendra Mandrupkar

BookLeaf Publishing

India | USA | UK

Made with ❤ on the BookLeaf Publishing Platform
www.bookleafpub.in
www.bookleafpub.com

Dedication

To my family, my haven and my harbor. You were the comforting ears that first embraced my tales, the enthusiastic chorus that lifted my voice, and the quiet assurance that fueled my creative spirit. Thank you for your enduring faith in the whispers of my soul.

Preface

Poetry often finds its way into the quiet corners of life between a sunrise seen from a office window, a cup of tea before a morning meeting, or a stray thought during a long commute. While machines may drive my workdays, it is words that drive my heart.

This is my second collection of poems, a continuation of that gentle dialogue between life and language. These verses are simple, unguarded, and honest. This book includes poem which doesn't wear any heavy metaphors and also doesn't try to impress; The poems just want to sit with you for a moment, just like a old friend!
Whether you're a seasoned reader of poetry or someone just wandering into these pages out of curiosity, I hope you find a reflection, a smile, or maybe a memory waiting to be remembered. These poems were born in stolen moments, and I offer them to you without boundaries of genre, age, or interpretation.
After all, poetry doesn't ask who you are it simply asks if you feel.

So come, turn the page. Let's read, feel, and wander together.
- Shardul Narendra Mandrupkar

Acknowledgements

Writing this book gives me joy of sharing my journey and I am deeply grateful to all the beautiful people who have walked along with me.

First, to my family, I thank you for being my unwavering support. Your belief, love and patience have carried me through every moment of doubt. You're the motivation and heart of everything I do.

To my friends, I thank you for your honest feedback and constant encouragement.

You might not realize it but your words, laughter and sometimes just presence, helped me shape these poems in ways I can't describe.

To my colleagues, I thank you for the hidden and unexpected inspiration that often came from our conversations. You may not realise it, but your perspectives pushed me to see the world in new ways.

And finally, to you, the readers, I thank you for picking up this book.

Your connection to these poems and their words, however brief or deep, makes every line of poem worth writing.

This book exists because of you. For you, I hope it brings a little light, a enlighting thought or a smile to your day!

1. The Journey

Encompassing experiences with mindfulness,
one place to another, like life enhances.

Road that leads to new heights,
turns that provide new insights.

Pressure of new city in the brain,
but excitement leads that pain.

From old city to distant lands,
A journey starts with impatient hands.

The way ahead, a curving path,
with old recaps, happiness to craft.

From vibrant towns and farms so green,
A world of amuses, egar to be seen.

For every inch of road, a story told,
Of new explorations, dreams unfold.

With every turn, a new Wonder,
Under the Boundless sky, a new thunder.

One journey ends, and a new journey stay,
Yet the memories of past cities, stay along the way.

2. God is Suffering

God is suffering, in the sorrows unseen,
In the smiles of broken, the silences inbetween.
In the hunger of a begger and cries on their road,
In the rain of troubles and problems on load!

God is suffering, in the darkness of mind,
In the wounded heart and soul so unkind.
In the unuttered calls of those who lost,
In the evening of nothing and what cost?

God is suffering, with no light in hand,
In the dark soul and No one understand.
In the peace vanished, loud noises in air,
Keeping mum, pleading the one,
In the shadows of despair.
God is suffering!

3. The Evening

Red mixed yellow and pink like denizen
the colors of happiness spread across horizon.

The sun started to packing things up,
darkness took then next gear up!

Beautiful mornings often start with amaze,
but evenings start with little amusing craze.
Small small moments cherishing happiness,
closing office shutters without any sadness.

The sun set view, shining in eyes,
forgetting all when what and whys!
Pushing through the day, ending struggles,
Sleeping thoughts and evening prayers!

Free and fair, breezy but sweet,
evening colors shatters
and day ends neat!

4. Father

In the shadows of fear and fight so real,
he stands with us even when dark makes deal!
He backs us to do extra than ordinary,
he pushes us to make works Visionary!

He stands tall even in thunder storms,
he always keeps us good and warm.
we fight with his courage taken as loan,
we challenge life with his words token!

We go to war, thinking he is supporting back,
with him beside, there is no set back.
He sacrifices his world, for our love,
we still deny his ocean size heart we dove!

One day, we call and he disappears,
we cry soul out but he never reappears!
we lose him someday, the fear stays,
Hug him still you can count your days!

5. Stress

Heart beating, racing the rush,
brain veins popping like a water in flood,
blood speeds through body in a flash,
The stress peaks and tension bash.

Feelings are just some thoughts with no value,
and words are like journey with no venue.

it's all about mind in a confused state,
True or false and how both are met.

Surrendered body to a devils will,
situation when one put himself to kill.

They said, 'Time will definitely save'
but mind said, 'If so, then how stress will pave'
Stressful life and no time to live,
Work like donkey and no
good to believe.

6. Pressure

In room where screens glow,
where code has endless flow,
An engineer, both egar and bright,
Politics, battles silent, out of sight

The ticking timeline, restless chase,
Deadlines appear, there's no embrace.
Emails and pings, demands on peak,
But on the checklist, there's no tick.

In networks mixes, problems hide,
In codes's depth, Answers bide.
each bug a crossword, each fix is feat
Yet stress and tension, they never beat.

Tea and coffee, the nights so long,
the wish to sleep must be strong.
But in the problems, no answers beside,
Balance of mind, there solution reside.

Must take deep breath and listen my friend,
Let not your mind and hear bend.
At last, eventually the screen will die out,
Peace of mind, thats what to look out.

7. The White Collar Gangsters

They walk in silence, but very fast,
they look everywhere and quickly grasp.

Clean and shaved, combed hairs,
they even wear tie, like anybody cares!

Their confidence lies in the ironed cloth,
their passion stays in the financial growth!

They shout on you with words that hurt,
they pinch the soul and throw in dirt!

Their truth is a lie we all have to agree,
Their face also lies, no one will disagree!

White Coller Gangsters is their name,
they are called as boss, but Don is their fame!

8. An Empty Desk

A friend of mine, leaving his seat,
called me for tea and something sweet!

A smile on his face, like hiding something,
his mouthful of thanks, that was everything!

It was still mid day and I saw him leave,
he was standing at the gate with a relief!

I looked and smiled like I didn't care,
I wondered how will it brake our pair.

My friend settled all and left on his last day,
empty desk was asking, how long will I stay!

9. His Pain

He called, numb in words, he cried!
My friend was in trouble, to understand I tried.

He was in pain, so much of stress,
I couldn't understand, how much was the mess.

Later in the time everybody forgot,
he was there alone, fighting with the odd.

He knocked every door, Broke every wall,
all ways closed, none heard the call!

He then fought with himself in mind,
his mind might have told him to grind.

He started with new courage and strength,
pulled all strings and ran through the length.

He failed in that even after struggle,
failure became his mate, with it he snuggled!

Suddenly a morning, people got a call,
he died by pain which everyone could recall!

10. Missing Rain

it was kind, it was soothing and cold,
suddenly it stopped, move so bold.

summer of '24, went like a hot oven,
black magic done, by witches full coven.

What part of day was not with hot sun?
we all were crying for mercy, atleast for fun?

Outside was like sun raising coup,
two minutes out, felt like toast with blood soup.

Inside the house, it felt really safe,
but, sweat was reminding that it was all fake.

Praying god for rain to pour,
why our lives made so sour.

Then atlast it came running down,
making us realise, be there no frown!

11. Who is "Wife"

In her Presence, a heaven is found,
with her words, a soothing sound.
her smile, like a tune so sweet,
lightens my heart very very neat!

In her eyes, resides star's shine,
presenting care that's truly divine.
Her touch, a easing balm to strife,
In her, I discovered a partner for life.

Through hurdles, together we stand,
Side by side, alongside, we withstand.
With her company, I feel like whole,
Feels like she is hook to my soul.

Wife, companion and a true best friend,
With you, my journey has no end.
With you I see myself happier,
You and I, together strong forever.

12. Invisible Pain

Hit by bus, blood everywhere, Chaos and sound, but pain
was invisible!

Crying baby beside a dying mother, Shouting brother
calling to another,
everywhere death silent in the air,
but pain was invisible!

Someone in shock and puking glass, visible cut throat
soaked in red bath, closed eyes,
darkness everywhere,
but pain was invisible!

Somewhere at a distance watching at this crime, the
man's heart with a throbbing and beating ache,
fear everywhere,
but pain was invisible!

13. Unfortunate silence

The night, cool breezes, empty sky
and unfortunate silence!

Evening's shine lost in dust,
noise and vibrations all in waste,
peoples voices down to mute,
The night, owls, sky lights
and unfortunate silence!

Money spent on lights,
colourful delights, all the shouts and un-necessary fights,
The night, chirping crickets, dogs crying
and unfortunate silence!

Brain filled thoughts, worry about future,
no one to talk and punctured mind,
The night, howling wolves, upset nature
and unfortunate silence!

14. Step out of the Matrix

The clouds of doubts in surrounding air,
the benefit of clarification not so clear,
beliefs so fake but near to the truth,
honesty selling on every toll booth!

Working like slaves, naming us employees,
pressure building up, darkness in the skys.
One to another, everyone is crushed,
no one alive to see how it all mushed.

Perspectives of all, together in sync,
point of view of one, everytime shrink.
if one is awake, he makes everyone rotten,
although individuals, together forgotten!

Possibility of doubt crushed on every step,
reasonable situation worsened without prep.
Step out of the matrix, is call of today,
otherwise you will be killed everyday!

15. The night and its magic

The night and its magic, no one awake and nothing
tragic!

Beneath the velveteen cloak of night,
the world is quite and enveloped in glow of moonlight!
No footsteps near and no voices around,
just the twinkle of stars sky bound!

In the night shadows, all secrets are kept,
as the world peacefully slept!
The night, a paper for dreams to unfurl,
where magic happens, in each twirl!

Through the silence, the soul takes flight,
in the arms of wonderful night.
No sorrows, no worries on the way,
just the calm mind with the end of day!

16. We Want a Summer Break Too!

We also need a summer break,
At least a month's leave to escape the year-long ache.

Not like work-from-home with endless calls,
We need free time, no more meeting brawls.

A relaxed life with afternoon naps so sweet,
Just like school's summer break—oh, what a treat!

Let results come, we are all set,
Though we consider work as exam with no regret!

No work stress chasing us around,
No deadlines, no office bound.

No AC, no towering walls,
Just open skies and nature's calls.

Playing all day till hunger strikes,
Mango pulp at home—oh, what delight!

No fridge, just cool earthen pots,
No ice cream, no soda shots—
A simple ice candy will hit the spot.

For a whole month, office doors will stay unseen,
No work, no laptop charging routine.

Oh God, just grant this one request,
Even if childhood never returns, that's fine at best.
Just give us a summer break once more,
And childhood will follow, like before!

17. Let's meet again, just like before

Let's meet again, just like before,
Like childhood days we still adore.
When summers came with endless cheer,
Let's bring those golden moments near.

Vacation time, pure fun, no rules,
No books, just games and breaking tools.
Let's laugh and play the whole day through,
Like old times, with our crazy crew.

We'd chase the sun, we'd raise some noise,
Like wild and carefree girls and boys.
With mangoes ripe and aamras sweet,
And ice cream dreams before we sleep.

We'd storm the town in wild delight,
Then fall asleep by calm moonlight.
So what I say, both loud and true—
Let's meet again, like we used to do.

We'd lie on rooftops, watch the skies,
And dream of stars with wondering eyes.
We'd talk of space and flying high,
And build our castles in the sky.

We'd rush to gardens, eat our fill,
Of bhel and puris, what a thrill!
We'd slide until our backs turned sore,
Then yawn and nap, and dream some more.

Let's wander like we used to then,
Let's be those kids just once again.
I say this now with heart so pure—
Let's meet again, just like before.

18. Storms of the Heart

Like strokes upon a sapphire sky,
The clouds invade, they rush, they fly—
Unseasoned storms in winter's grace,
Uncalled, they came and found their place.

Who will say what stirred the air?
A stranger wind is blowing there.
The seasons turned, the cycle broke,
And all the world felt disarrayed and woke.

The rain, it has its nature true—
To fall, to weep, like I now do.
My heart is tangled in this rain,
Its secrets soaked in silent pain.

Just yesterday, a gentle breeze,
Now storms have stripped away my peace.
A fleeting season of the soul,
Now cold winds howl and take their toll.

Waves once calm now crash and cry,
The tempests rage, the past says bye.
So tell me now, with all your art—
What storm is brewing in your heart?

19. That's What Joy Feels Like

What is joy, we often ask,
A mystery wrapped in every task.
But truth is simple, clear, and bright,
It's hidden in the daily light.
Yet somehow, we forget it so,
While chasing dreams that come and go.

Waking up as morning glows,
Beside the stove where warm steam flows.
Brushing teeth in that rising heat,
That cozy warmth—now that's joy's beat.

Joy's not far, it's always near,
In moments small, it feels sincere.
Not in gold or in the grand,
But in the simple, close at hand.
Yes, that's what joy feels like...
That's what joy feels like.

Bathing with your favorite soap,
The breeze that hugs you as you cope.
Still damp, you stand beneath the sun,
And feel its touch—soft, golden, fun.

Hot upma fresh from mom's old pan,
A hurried bite before it can
Go cold—your tongue feels that little sting,
And joy just dances in everything.

Your boss is out, your day feels light,
Clouds roll in, the sky turns night.
You crave a chai you didn't plan,
And smile at life's sweet sleight of hand.

The lunchbox smell before you see
What's inside—it sets you free.
You lift the lid, and there it lies—
Your favorite dish, a sweet surprise.

Heading home while daylight fades,
The sunset's art in golden shades.
A line of verse flows through your head—
A poem blooms where words were dead.

Joy's not far, it's in your day,
In silent smiles, in simple play.

A morning breeze, a noonday bite,
A fading sun, a verse at night.
Yes, that's what joy feels like...
That's what joy feels like.

20. Poet's Story

A delight of life, less of a burden,
writing is a hobby, but a joy for certain.
It is an art that makes a heart full,
even less money but wins love eventful.

A poet is a man, who express his heart,
he declares himself hurt, to save his art.
A poem is a way to express every good,
love, hate, anger, to express every mood.

Every book is a story, a writer tells,
he pours soul and enrich all tales.
Every book is a movie, that runs readers minds,
here and there, every page that it binds.

A reader saves the world, a writer encourages,
A reader fights them all, which writer emerges.
A reader just read, but writer lives,
A reader's imagination, it all writer leaves.

This book is same, for reader's amuse,
its a tour of misery, happiness and excuse.
The Poet's Story, the journey it holds,
Poet's life and its turns it unfolds!

21. The end

What does end really mean?
is it just bye or good bye so keen?
is end really stops all progress?
or end is just, starting call of distress?

Does end is just some words we say?
Is it not the only truth of the day?
End is somewhere, tearing all apart,
It is all a circle, where it ends before a start!

End is a pause, not a full stop,
end is a comma, before a new drop.
This is not end, but a start,
A new beginning, from the heart!